Hi, I'm Ricky. I am 3. I
have a food allergy.

peanuts in shell

I can't eat peanuts or tree nuts. I would get really sick.

peanut butter

peanuts

cashews

mixed nuts

almonds

trail mix

pistachios

walnuts

Please note: not all tree nuts are shown here.

Lots of foods have peanuts or tree nuts in them, even if you can't see them.

They are
NOT safe
for me to
eat.

So Mommy and Daddy
check my food to keep me
safe.

I always ask Mommy
or Daddy before I eat
something.

So at a party I say, "Mommy,
is that safe to eat?" She says,
"No, but we brought safe
cupcakes for you."

My cupcakes have lots of icing and safe sprinkles.

I love the swings at the park.
Mmm, I see candy on the
ground.

Big sister Annie yells "NO! That candy is not safe for you!"

I love to go
on picnics.
"Mommy,
can I have some chips?"
Mommy says "Yes, they are
safe. I'll get you a bowl."

We finish our snack. Then
we go play.

I like going food shopping
with Daddy. I pick out the
apples.

"Daddy, can I have this cereal?" Daddy says, "Let me check it... Yes! That is safe for you."

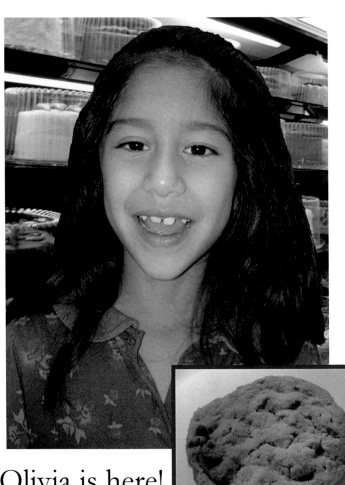

Olivia is here!
She has a big
cookie. Daddy says, "No
sharing cookies." We don't
know if it is safe for me.

16

"Daddy, can I have that candy?" Daddy says "No, not safe" to some treats I really want.

Sometimes, I get really mad.

But I have my own safe
snacks and treats Mommy
and Daddy make for me.

Mommy and Annie just made cookies.

"Can I eat this cookie, Daddy?" Daddy says, "Yes, let's all have cookies!"

First Tips for Parents

• Get a referral to a board-certified allergist. An allergist is specially trained to handle your child's serious food allergy.

• Always carry your child's emergency epinephrine medicine (EpiPen® or Twinject™, for example).

• Always read ingredient labels. Avoid any food containing peanuts or tree nuts.

• Call the company if you are not sure the food is safe. The company's phone number may be on the food package.

• If there are no ingredients listed, then the answer is "No, you can't have that."

• Avoid foods that were processed on the same equipment as peanut or tree nut products.

Tips for Parents at Home

• Make your home a "safe zone". This means no peanut or tree nut products **anywhere** in your home.

• Remind your relatives and friends before they come to visit. Even with reminders, food your visitors bring may not be safe for your child. [Read more on the www.PeanutAllergy.Com discussion boards about how others handle this situation.]

• Be prepared for an emergency. With your allergist's help, write down an action plan that lists the steps to take if your child is exposed to peanuts or tree nuts. [Use the Food Allergy Action Plan from www.foodallergy.org.]

• Your action plan should include when and how to use your child's emergency epinephrine medicine. Post the plan on your refrigerator.

• Show your child's babysitter which foods are safe for your child. Show the babysitter the action plan and how to use your child's emergency epinephrine medicine.

Tips for Parents When Going Out

• Teach your child to ask you before eating anything when out. This may take a while for your child to learn.

• Plan ahead! Always carry a safe snack for your child. Bring a safe cupcake or treat for your child if going to a party.

• Many restaurants are not safe for your child. Call ahead and ask questions like "What kind of oil do you use when making French fries?"

• When planning playgroup outings, remind the other parents about your child's allergy. Your child will be safer if your outing is free of peanut and tree nut products.

• When choosing a preschool, ask careful questions about the school's willingness to work with food-allergic kids. Can they create a safe place for your child? Can they follow your child's written action plan?

Learn More

• The more you know, the safer your child is! Get educated through these wonderful groups. Read the books they recommend.

• Contact the Food Allergy & Anaphylaxis Network at 800-929-4040 or www.foodallergy.org. Receive their newsletters and allergy alert messages.

• Join www.PeanutAllergy.Com for important advice on keeping your child safe. They provide updated information, education and personal assistance. Visit their website or call them at 207-766-5292.

• Consider getting a MedicAlert® Bracelet for your child. Call 888-633-4298 or view at www.medicalert.org.

Notes